BELIEVE IN YOUR SELF

A self discovery book
By Loren Hart

A COMPREHENSIVE GUIDE TO GROWING YOUR SELF-CONFIDENCE

BELIEVE IN YOURSELF

BELIEVE IN YOURSELF

Copyright 2022 by My Stars Books
All Rights Reserved

No part of this book may be produced or transmitted in any form by any means whatsoever without express written permission from the author, except in the case of brief quotations embodied in critical articles and reviews.

Please refer all pertinent questions to the publisher.

My Stars Books
THE SHELF WITH BEAUTIFUL STORIES

/MyStarsBooks

/MyStarsBooks

Thank you for your recent purchase.

Positive feedback from our valued customers really helps us to continue attracting more great customers such as yourself and to improve our work.
If you wouldn't mind leaving an online review section, we would really appreciate that.

BELIEVE IN YOURSELF

TABEL OF CONTENTS

Disclaimer ....
Introductory ....
Chapter 1: A Step Toward Self-Confidence ....
Chapter 2: A Philosophy to Boost Your Self-Belief ....
Chapter 3: Building Self-Esteem and Confidence ....
Chapter 4: Why People Lack Self-Belief ....
Chapter 5: Thoughts on Increasing Self-Belief ....
Chapter 6: What to Do to Increase Your Self-Confidence ....
Chapter 7: Advice on How to Improve Your Self-Confidence ....
Chapter 8: Develop Your Own Self-Belief ....

BELIEVE IN YOURSELF

DISCLAIMER

The sole intent of this ebook is to provide information. This booklet has been meticulously researched and fact-checked to the best of our ability.

However, there can be grammatical or substance errors. Additionally, the material in this ebook is only current as of publication. So, rather than serving as the sole source, this ebook should only be used as a reference.

This ebook aims to educate readers. The content in this e-book is not guaranteed to be accurate by the author or the publisher, and they are not liable for any mistakes omissions.

Regarding any loss or damage caused or said to have been caused directly indirectly by this ebook, the author and publisher are not liable or responsible to any person or entity.

INTRODUCTORY

The main concern when addressing the growth of self-confidence in a person who, for a long time, felt that his self-worth was lacking is how to acquire self-confidence.

It goes without saying that those who are more self-assured can handle themselves better than those who are less self-assured. They are the leaders of society, the achievers, and the spotlight-seekers. They are well-groomed, talk clearly, and have both subtle and overt impacts on others. In other words, these are individuals who care and can be seen from a distance.

Self-assured persons are sometimes incredibly well-liked by society. It can be because of their charisma or the fact that they are naturally highly friendly. There are, however, those self-assured people who can make a room feel lighter by simply departing.

These two instances of confidence are significantly different from one another. One destroys a person's credibility and the other intensifies his personality. And it goes without saying that you would not want the results of being overconfident in yourself, which would be that others stop seeing you as effective and start seeing you as an inconvenience in their daily lives.

Self-assurance originates from the inside. The outside stimulus could be beneficial, but would still come down to knowing yourself and using that understanding to obtain assurance.

BELIEVE IN YOURSELF

You must understand that your strengths should not limit you and your weaknesses shouldn't devastate you if you want to develop self-confidence. Instead, make use of all of these things to create a personality that will benefit both you and everyone around you.

The Oracle of Delphi exclaims, "Know thyself!" Despite the fact that the statement may have been spoken thousands of years ago, it is definitely true that we can still employ wisdom, so they say.

Gain confidence and awareness of oneself. Recognize, however, that you are the only source of knowledge. You must therefore face the fact that the demons of low self-confidence will continue to haunt you unless you accept your imperfections and perfection.

However, if you know too much about yourself, it could be dangerous. The foundations of self-control are still developing. Since you do not yet have control, you might be consumed by your own flows since you would be exposed to your flaws. Though rumination, where you appear to go around in your circle of thoughts about your losses and failures regardless of your achievements, is directly related to this disease.

Another risk of losing self-control when working on your confidence is that you can become so self-assured that you lose sight of the true benefits of feeling good about yourself. You would eventually fail again as a result of this, or worse.

Knowing yourself is one thing that may either be risky or beneficial. People frequently become aware of how amazing their invention was through self-awareness. They learn to value their skills and qualities, which are undoubtedly as unique as those that may be shared by others. It is true that each of us is distinct. By carefully examining

BELIEVE IN YOURSELF

…r abilities and limitations, we can recognize the distinctive characteristics that make us …ecial. Our innate gifts, which increase our sense of increased self-worth, are how our …dividuality is expressed. We can see our individuality in the potential we can choose to …erlook or maximize.

Unless you learn to reflect on who you are and are aware of who you really are, these facts will remain concealed from you.

CHAPTER 1: A STEP TOWARD SELF-CONFIDENCE

Every endeavor must begin somewhere. If you don't start updating your se assurance, you'll have to suffer through countless hours of the very your greatest wor is a lack of confidence.

Our self-confidence is the culmination of all of our responses to the experienc that life has given us, as well as how we have followed the advice of the more experienc members of our community and how others perceive us. Many things are contributors our unique understanding of confidence.

How well we expect ourselves and the situations in our lives to be one of t determining factors. Many people have a tendency to set themselves up disappointment by doing this. Their losses become so excruciatingly painful along t process that individuals finally begin to experience the repercussions of diminish confidence.

Others, on the other hand, like to play it safer and set more realistic objectiv that are simpler to meet. Furthermore, knowing that they are capable of completi something helps these people because accomplishments significantly contribute to t growth of self-confidence.

It's all in the mind, as you may have already heard. And we can genuinely cla that everything is all in the head in regard to numerous psychological and emotio disorders. The antidote may as well originate from the same source since they are root in and grow out of the mind.

BELIEVE IN YOURSELF

You can always train your body to feel how you want it to or how you don't want to. You can stifle feelings, which will encourage feelings to manifest. Let's say you want to hate yourself because you are inadequate. You will only produce genuine hatred and reduced self-esteem if you force yourself to accept that hatred and that you are truly convinced that you are unworthy.

Most of us speak without thinking when we do. We occasionally forget to check ourselves for the things our subconscious mind is registering.

You may not have said it on purpose recently, but because you are accustomed to. As you say to yourself, "I am a loser," or "I'm not deserving of anything," you could as well convince your subconscious that these are the facts. Many people still hold these claims to be true as we speak.

They are more than just words. They really exist, and they will delve far into your subconscious mind before integrating them into your existence. There is no way that you can avoid believing in these if you believe in their polar opposite.

The ability to believe in oneself is essential for developing self-confidence. Everything you decide to believe will be accepted as true. As a result, all you need to do is change the values you want. If not, no amount of waiting will change you. The drive must originate with you. Though suggestions may come from outside sources, ultimately the battle will be fought by you and only you.

Changes have to start with you. You may start by telling yourself things like, "You are terrific," because you really are a great person who just needs to have your talents discovered. Or "you are lovely" (because, whether you believe it or not, every one of us was exquisitely designed to reflect glory on our Creator).

BELIEVE IN YOURSELF

You won't be able to maintain your insanity for very long about lacking confidence.

You must find a way to alter your viewpoints and live a different life that anticipates greater things.

CHAPTER 2: A PHILOSOPHY TO BOOST YOUR SELF-BELIEF

Everybody is proud of the possessions we have. Each of us has become an achiever on our own, regardless of the successes we have had or the current standard of life we have been able to produce.

However, any of us may have disputed this reality. But as you can see, anyone can accomplish anything if they put their hearts into it and make up their minds to do it. Nobody is denied the chance to rejoice in life's victories. The only ones who suffer are those who deny themselves these gifts. Who are they among you?

Leave your response open-ended and then mumble it to yourself. Make sure you modify things for the better regardless of the outcome.

If you can claim to be sufficiently confident, that's great! Do not, however, content yourself with what is adequate. There will always be gaps, so stop looking for methods to do better.

However, if your response was "no," go on immediately. You would undoubtedly regret everything when you left this world if you wasted your life listening to negative whimpers.

Imagine how horrible it would be to know you have all you needed to succeed but dared not use it.

BELIEVE IN YOURSELF

A baby eagle once lived in a community of hens and was nurtured there. He wa[s] brought up thinking he was a chicken and was oriented to live like one. He has bee[n] admiring the eagles' magnificent performance as they hover in the air for a while.

He longs to have been born like these flying eagles every time he stands in aw[e] of them. Even if his heart still yearns to soar to the heights eagles reach, he dared n[ot] stretch his wings. He died a chicken, always yearning to become one of those to who[m] he genuinely belonged since he was never able to realize his potential and true nature.

We are all eagles, one and all. To the full extent of our abilities, we can all fly. W[e] will always be constrained by our inability to rise above our circumstances and becom[e] the true individuals we were intended to be unless we spread our wings and dare to fi[nd] our true selves.

We could all have led happy and contented lives if we had only realized the eag[le] that is dormant inside of us.

Each of us was born with the ability to succeed. The Universe is simply too goo[d] for us and she took the time to make sure we have everything we needed to soar. Do[n't] blow this opportunity by packing your back with heavy things that would make yo[u] unable to fly.

Think of yourself as an eagle that has emerged from the muck of being a chicke[n]. It is intended to butcher chickens. Similar to this, if we decide to act like chickens, we w[ill] have to face the fact that our goals will not be achieved. That is, to praise the Univers[e] who has cared for us and provided for all of our needs.

BELIEVE IN YOURSELF

Live a life devoid of the destructive aspects of the culture, like an eagle chicken. like a bird of prey and let your confidence work for you. You can benefit from being a powerful being.

Take flight like an eagle and live a life free of the destructive customs of the chickens. Be like a bird of prey and capitalize on your assurance. Being a powerful beast can benefit you.

CHAPTER 3: BUILDING SELF-ESTEEM AND CONFIDENCE

Optimism! Everything depends on how positively we perceive ourselves, the world around us, and life itself. We are obligated to enjoy life as every man should as long we have faith in any potential for goodness.

Unfortunately, a lot of us have a hard time seeing the bright side of a life fill with hardships, sickness, and challenges. It stands to reason that happiness witho pleasure would not be recognized. If all we know is joy, we cannot experience pain. If were always happy, tears would be worthless. If we did not occasionally fall flat on o faces, confidence would not be recognized. We have the freedom to achieve anything desire in life, which is a wonderful privilege.

We must begin laying our foundations as soon as possible to prevent losi priceless opportunities that will never come again. While a moment that has passed lost forever, your light will continue to shine long after you are gone.

We would be able to recognize the extent of our potential if we were optimis about life. Everyone has an equal chance to be noticed, yet many of us never get our f share of the spotlight because we give up before the battle ever starts.

You need to have the courage to share what the world has to give. Nothing, r even the horrible demons of low confidence, should prevent you from living your life.

Those who have risked life are those who are self-assured enough. Sometim we simply have to take chances in order to learn what is in store for us. However, taki

...ances calls for a lot of self-confidence. You would be like a warrior who has lost his ...mor without this.

We were given all the talents we would need later in life from the moment of our ...rth. One such ability is the capacity to meet obstacles head-on and to do so with faith—...nfidence in both ourselves and faith in the One who created us all.

Even though it seems like our friend is much luckier than us, we all had an equal ...ance to establish our sense of self.

We frequently believe that life is unjust when, in truth, it isn't. Each of us has both ...essings and challenges in equal measure. It all comes down to how we see the world ...d how we handle situations.

The same is true of self-esteem and confidence. Many of us assume that the man ...e look up to shares many of life's gifts because he is more articulate and self-assured ...an most of us can handle himself better in public, and can face the world. Keep in mind ...at before he even got there, he had to overcome obstacles that boosted his sense of ...lf-worth and confidence. Only if we have enough faith in ourselves may any of us ...come that man.

To develop solid foundations for our self-esteem and self-confidence, we simply ...ed to uncover our own enlightenment.

Before we can accept the support that comes from without, we first need to make ...anges within. If you, yourself, do not want to accept this one basic reality, outside ...inforcement cannot help you realize how valuable and lovely you were created.

BELIEVE IN YOURSELF

Don't hesitate to assist in your own self-discovery; it will be one of the most rewarding endeavors you ever do.

CHAPTER 4: WHY PEOPLE LACK SELF-BELIEF

No single thing may be regarded as the source of all other factors. Where does poor self-esteem come from?

Actually, the reason we are struggling to find and address prior mistakes and deficiencies is because of their accumulation. It is the result of our inability to identify our true selves and the obstacles to our own development.

Clearly, having low self-confidence is restricting. It would force us to ignore our natural abilities and view our failures as preliminary setbacks. It would keep us confined to our familiar surroundings, where nothing could possibly go wrong or make us look foolish. The comfort zones will then convince us that we shouldn't leave its perimeter since disappointments and setbacks await us there.

However, even when we warn ourselves about how difficult and chaotic things could become, we must continue to resist giving in to the inner critic that lives inside of us. At the very least, we must vanquish it and demonstrate our superiority to the world.

When we are young, low self-confidence begins to develop. Unfortunately, a lot of us have relatives, acquaintances, professors, and foes who are more aware of our flaws than our strengths. They would criticize us for our errors and destroy our motivation. Although they may not have spoken these things directly to our faces, their gestures and sneers are more than enough to persuade us that we are losers. Perhaps you are surrounded by harsh judgmental eyes that are blind to flaws.

BELIEVE IN YOURSELF

Or perhaps you are the underling of a brother who excels in school, which would explain why everyone is so focused on him and frequently ignores you. People probably take care of you when they think you are unable to take care of yourself.

These are all subtly triggering situations that would eventually cause you to lose confidence.

You would quickly discover that you are truly unable of doing things while reality, you have gifts beyond your own estimation due to such lousy examples and lack of attention given to you.

Your adherence to their views would lead you to blame yourself for all of your shortcomings. At times, you might even persuade yourself that you share some of the blame for the shortcomings of those you interact with frequently.

Sweeping generalizations will become routine for you as a child. Even without the support of the twisted people around you, you will persuade yourself of how foolish you are.

Additionally, as the process advances, you will learn to dismiss the blatant unfavorable accusations made against you by others. And to make matters worse on top of all of your other issues, you would come to think that life is nothing but setbacks and failures.

Your confidence in yourself has already been severely damaged. In order to avoid this self-tormenting course of life, you would not dare attempt to settle your sense of inner conflict. Thoughtful individuals and solutions would come to you. However, your responses would either be to ignore them completely or to push them away.

BELIEVE IN YOURSELF

If you keep going through this phase, you'll soon realize that the solution to your lack of confidence is right in front of you, but because you're all so lost in your own world, seeing the issue would be next to impossible. Unless you encounter a miracle that completely changes your life.

CHAPTER 5: THOUGHTS ON INCREASING SELF-BELIE[F]

Be not deceived. Even the most self-assured people experience insecurities, and even the most skilled people have flaws.

Even if we may have fantasized about being the flawless individuals we admire [in] others, we must realize that nothing is perfect. No matter how well-thought-out o[ur] intentions were, things rarely go exactly as we would like them to in life. As long as w[e] continue to put effort into reaching our goals, we won't let them slip through our finge[rs]. However, action is required to make things happen. And those who are confident [in] themselves did not just happen to have these qualities.

The most attractive people do not just happen, according to a famous autho[r]. Before individuals completely comprehend the depth of their value, they must fi[rst] experience hardship, pain, defeat, struggle, and loss.

Every person is made for success, acclaim, and renown. The capability to bri[ng] confidence in oneself is a quality that each of us possesses. similar to with regard [to] everything else, we are on par with the person seated next to us. The difference, thoug[h,] is in how each of us approaches the skills we were given on a personal level.

The origins of our early self-confidence were in our love of fashion. The metho[d] of upbringing, the opportunities that shaped us into the people that we are, and how [we] responded to the difficulties we faced.

We are all familiar with how it feels to be humiliated or encouraged. We begin [to] make interpretations of the events that happen to us at a very young age. If as childr[en] e didn't because of factors like inadequate or wrong supervision, bad role models, and sufficient understanding, it's possible that the subsequent stages of our lives will epend on how these earlier ones went.

But maturity comes with age. And maturity emerges from the situations we are ncountering. The best teachers we have are our experiences, as we know them. If we on't learn from the experiences we have, we'll keep running into the same problems ntil we can figure out where we went wrong. We, therefore, have no justification for hy we weren't given the opportunity to get better with each event.

You see, developing self-confidence just requires maturation. You won't nderstand that life is more than just mediocre living if you let the concept of failing to icceed and receive accolades make you complacent.

Regardless of our past self-confidence, everyone can increase it. The present is that matters. You will undoubtedly go closer to developing self-confidence if you take ock of who you are and feel that you are capable of being anything and everything.

There are many actions you can take to boost your self-confidence. The goal is to lopt the mindset that anyone can achieve anything, as well as the conviction that you n be anyone and whatever you put your mind to being.

If all else fails, think back to the times when you felt good because you were able accomplish something by having a positive self-perception. In this manner, you'll be spired to improve into the person you've always desired to be

CHAPTER 6: WHAT TO DO TO INCREASE YOUR SELF CONFIDENCE

Large changes result from small adjustments. Everything comes down to a single concept that would change the way you see yourself.

Do you recall a moment when you were certain you had done something, b[ut] then someone commented on how poorly it had gone? Remember when you we[re] struggling to do your task effectively and someone told you that you would never g[et] promoted?

Do you remember when you decided to run a mile and people teased you f[or] having such an ambitious goal? Recall all those occasions. They all stemmed from t[he] pessimistic commentary that served no purpose other than to crush the optimistic spi[rit] that tells you "you can."

Positivity and self-confidence go hand in hand. You can at least convince yours[elf] that you can do and influence events if you think well of yourself, examine all the goo[d] qualities you possess, and weigh their value against the ones you lack.

Being realistic in your expectations prevents you from having unrealistically hi[gh] expectations. Setting achievable goals that you can achieve without limiting your abiliti[es] is essential for increasing self-confidence and a positive attitude.

Typically, we tend to overestimate things when we set out to do something, a[nd] have goals that go beyond what we can now accomplish. We assert that th[is] would motivate us to put up double the effort. But what we are failing to see is that on[ce] we fall short of our own expectations as much as those of the audience that is watching we will lose motivation to try something new.

You see, it wouldn't be horrible if we started out by setting reasonable expectations. Rather than ego-boosting, impractical objectives that would leave us disappointed and dismayed.

When you really want to feel good about yourself, keep in mind that our body's hormonal balance plays a major role in determining our level of self-confidence. As a result, you can change your mood by encouraging it. For example, if you remember clearly achieving something or having "cheerleaders" who encouraged you to do more, you can utilize those memories to control your emotions. If not, consider the times when you felt truly confident in yourself. Being in charge of your emotions and moods might help you feel more confident overall.

We have all been our own worst critics at some point in our lives. Unjustified critiques alter our general personal perceptions in addition to making us more susceptible to negative thinking.

Have you ever observed how we criticize ourselves without even being aware that we aren't allowed to say those things to others? More than we can think, we are tougher on ourselves. As a result, we feel disturbed and insecure with each critical comment this critic makes. It is like breaking down the fences we have long constructed in return for a few unfair criticisms that we hardly ever require.

Avoid making generalizations about yourself because doing so could eventually cause you to lose your positive self-image. Your self-confidence will significantly suffer if you start repeating the criticism you offer yourself.

BELIEVE IN YOURSELF

Destruction ultimately originates from within us. Others could counter that we are impacted by negativity from the outside world. True, but this won't have an impact on us until we let it in. So, all you need to do is fortify your basic foundations while building barriers against bad inputs.

CHAPTER 7: ADVICE ON HOW TO IMPROVE YOUR SELF-CONFIDENCE

We are all made of this thing called life, which is confidence. The distinction simply results from our comprehension and acceptance of reality.

Some people are simply better than others at understanding who they are and what they are capable of.

Everything depends on how we see ourselves, how we comprehend possibilities, and how effectively we can employ our perception and comprehension.

We believe that having self-confidence is something that everyone else has but ourselves, similar to having money. You see, life was intended to be equal from the beginning.

Simply put, inequality results from our perceptions of what we already have but fail to appreciate, as well as what others have that we desire.

Be kind to yourself. Do not deny oneself the pleasure of life. Make an assessment of oneself and avoid using justifications like "looks" while keeping your eyes off the gold mine that is your neighbor's fences existing on your own property.

Everyone and everything has a natural beauty that only we can remove. All of us have the ability to use or ignore our gifts of talent, skill, beauty, and amazement. The reality is that life has more to offer than mediocrity once we realize our potential.

BELIEVE IN YOURSELF

But there are a few things from which we must realize that we are prohibite[d]. However, these are offset by the fact that we have the capacity to thrive in other area[s]. We only need to discover our veins and fortes.

Our prior experiences might have a limit on our understanding. However, th[is] does not change the reality that if we merely make a small effort to cultivate positi[ve] perceptions of who we really are, we can broaden our perspective of ourselves. Keep [in] mind that our success or failure depends on the attitude we choose to adopt. It does[n't] imply that when a friend accomplishes something better, he takes credit for it from yo[ur] own talent bank. It simply implies that he was able to realize his strengths and use th[e] realization for his own benefit.

Self-assurance and the methods we use to boost them are generally only wh[en] we have the guts to try things that we initially seemed impossible we have within [us]. Sometimes, we miss the potential impact of seemingly simple things, that help in bring[ing] the splendors of assurance to us. Numerous strategies exist for helping us increase o[ur] confidence.

The practice of public speaking and writing as well as other linguistic sk[ills] enhancing Your ability to feel more self-aware will be greatly aided by relationshi[ps]. majority of us have been embarrassed in front of others. But after we overcome this fe[ar] we're probably going to learn more about our capacities later on. Additionally, you cou[ld] locate support from developing your innate talents, of self-confidence.

If, for example, you enjoy combining poetry and notes or have a natu[ral] inclination to become involved in music, you can assist prevent low confidence [by] channeling your interest toward more beneficial endeavors. You may attempt to wr[ite]

...usic so that people can enjoy your songs, or you could engage in poetry to bring out ...ur inner creativity.

You just need to be open to unlimited possibilities. Keep in mind that the only ...erson who could prevent you from growing and the only one who could sacrifice for ...ur pleasure is you. Make a choice: Will you be your biggest ally or enemy?

CHAPTER 8: DEVELOP YOUR OWN SELF-BELIEF

The main concern when addressing the growth of self-confidence in a person who, for a long time, felt that his self-worth was lacking is how to acquire self confidence.

It goes without saying that those who are more self-assured can handle themselves better than those who are less self-assured. They are the leaders of society, the achievers, and the spotlight-seekers. They are well-groomed, talk clearly, and have both subtle and overt impacts on others. In other words, these are individuals who can and can be seen from a distance.

Self-assured persons are sometimes incredibly well-liked by society. It can be because of their charisma or the fact that they are naturally highly friendly. There are, however, those self-assured people who can make a room feel lighter by simply departing.

It goes without saying that those who are more self-assured can handle themselves better than those who are less self-assured. They are the leaders of society, the achievers, and the spotlight-seekers. They are well-groomed, talk clearly, and have both subtle and overt impacts on others. In other words, these are individuals who can and can be seen from a distance.

Self-assured persons are sometimes incredibly well-liked by society. It can be because of their charisma or the fact that they are naturally highly friendly. There are, however, those self-assured people who can make a room feel lighter by simply departing.

BELIEVE IN YOURSELF

To get self-confidence, you must realize that your limitations must not limit you and your attributes must not destroy you. Instead, use all these factors to develop a personality that would be productive for you and all those that surround you.

"Know thyself!", says the Oracle at Delphi. Though this might have been said thousands of years ago, it is undeniably true that we still can use the wisdom it says.

Gain confidence and awareness of oneself. Recognize, however, that you are the only source of knowledge. You must therefore face the fact that the demons of low self-confidence will continue to haunt you unless you accept your imperfections and perfection.

However, if your foundation for self-control is not very well built, there is a significant risk in knowing too much about oneself. Since you do not yet have control, you might be consumed by your own flows since you would be exposed to your flaws. Thought rumination, where you appear to go around in your circle of thoughts about your losses and failures regardless of your achievements, is directly related to this disease.

Another risk of losing self-control when working on your confidence is that you can become so self-assured that you lose sight of the true benefits of feeling good about yourself. As we've already discussed, having too much confidence can be just as risky as having none at all. This would bring you back to mistakes, or even worse, your final ruin. Knowing yourself is one thing that may either be risky or beneficial.

People frequently become aware of how amazing their invention was through self-awareness. They learn to value their skills and qualities, which are undoubtedly as unique as those that may be shared by others. It is true that each of us is distinct.

BELIEVE IN YOURSELF

By carefully examining our abilities and limitations, we can recognize the distinctive characteristics that make us special. Our innate gifts, which increase our sense of increased self-worth, are how our individuality is expressed. We can see our individuality in the potential we can choose to overlook or maximize.

Unless you have learned to reflect on your existence and be aware of who you truly are, all of these facts will remain hidden from you.

www.ingramcontent.com/pod-product-compliance
Lightning Source LLC
Chambersburg PA
CBHW070341120526
44590CB00017B/2978